WALK THE BIBLE IN 30 DAYS

by

Robert Fetterhoff

To my precious bride, Roxanne, whose love for our Lord, courage and faithfulness in my absence, and unwavering prayer support made it possible for me to travel to the land I have grown to love.

And

To my Lord Jesus Christ, who left the glory of heaven to walk this earth and provide redemption for me through His finished work on the cross.

Table of Contents

Acknowledgments

To Pastor Jim Custer, friend and mentor, who introduced me to the spiritual richness of the lands of the Bible.

To Jack and Deb Miller and Emerson Stull, whose support enabled this book to become a reality.

To Vern and Mary Schlabach, who gave me permission to use some of their amazing photographs.

To Mark Curtis, Jane Mosier, Becky Chodzin, Johanna Stull Smith and Steve Knight, who proofread the entire manuscript and provided suggested corrections. Any lingering issues are the fault of this author.

To my son-in-law, Adam Kasper, for his suggestions for a cover design.

To my father and mother, Pastor Dean and Billie Fetterhoff, who taught me to love the Word of God and the Son of God since I was a child.

To my daughters and sons-in-law, Kristen and Jon Ekhoff, and Kara and Adam Kasper, who have brought me great joy, especially during our journeys to the Holy Land together.

To the hundreds of travelers who spent their time and money to travel with me and experience the places that help the Bible "come alive."

Without the help and encouragement of each of you, this book simply would not have been possible.

Foreword

IF FOLKS CAN'T TRAVEL TO ISRAEL - BRING ISRAEL TO THEM in a month's experience!!! How exciting. All they need is a good map of Israel, their personal copy of God's Word, and a quiet place to ingest devotional comments which you 'share There' each trip!

Those who 'have been There' can refresh their personal experiences with these materials and relive those moments with pictures which they took while visiting these Biblical places! Brilliant – and refreshing.

We both know that Israel is both a Biblical treasure house and a huge distraction for the serious traveler. There is SO much to see – the land, the stories of restored Israel in her Homeland, the battle with the marketplace and its zillions of 'take home to the friends' items, and the indescribable thrill of standing in the actual places where the 'Word was made flesh' and brought Heaven's graces to earthly people.

To sail in the same waters on which Peter actually walked –

To stand in the space where Jesus actually died –

To pray in the place where He sweat drops of blood

To stand on the same mountain where His feet will land when He returns with us –

I mean, those are incredible, mind-numbing, Faith-building, life changing moments!

Thanks, Bob, for creating this fresh way to narrow the distractions of travel and multiply the advantages for folks who yearn to imagine-feel-touch the anchors of our faith within their hearts and minds through His fingerprints in His Word and within His World.

Because of His Grace –

Pastor Jim Custer

Teaching Pastor

Grace Polaris Church

Westerville, OH

Introduction

"Welcome to Israel!"
Read Genesis 12:1-8

I NEVER GET TIRED OF SAYING THOSE WORDS! FOR MANY, A TRIP to Israel is a lifelong dream, an ambition that never dies in the heart of a child of God. For some, it represents years of hoping, saving and planning.

A trip to the Holy Land includes many surprises. I tell passengers, "When you travel internationally, expect the unexpected!" You never know when you will experience a flight delay, encounter some problem at a border crossing or adjust to a change in the itinerary. But one thing is certain – you will never be the same! Your hunger for the Written Word increases, your love for the Living Word comes alive, even your appreciation for fellow travelers develops.

For the next 30 days, you will read the lessons and applications God has provided me through more than 25 years of visiting the land of our Lord, including sites in both Israel and Jordan. These devotionals are organized largely around the chronology of the Bible. Therefore, we focus first on Old Testament accounts, then New Testament details. Of course, it's impossible to cover all the stories, so this will provide an overview of significant people and places.

At the beginning of each devotional, you will find a theme and Scripture reading chosen because of a significant event or character associated with that particular location. You will also find a prayer of reflection at the conclusion to each devotional. To benefit most from this book, please record your own thoughts and prayer in the section entitled, "My Prayer Journal."

These readings are designed to introduce you to four main characters of the Old Testament: Abraham, Moses, David and Daniel, who lived approximately 500 years apart. Later we turn our attention to John the Baptist, then the Lord Jesus, as we uncover God's plan of redemption for this world. Each reading provides an opportunity to gain greater clarity about the stories and events contained in the pages of the Scriptures. Every day provides one soul-stirring highlight after another!

One thing is certain – a trip to the Holy Land will change your life. You will never read the same Bible. It is my sincere prayer that these devotionals will give you a glimpse of what it's like to walk where Jesus walked, or perhaps rekindle a visit you enjoyed in the past. I've tried to capture the essence of the teaching and themes from each location, but the spiritual impact is best experienced in person!

May God bring His Word alive as you "Walk the Bible in 30 Days!"
In His Matchless Grace –
Pastor Bob Fetterhoff

DAY 1

Caesarea by the Sea

Theme: The Gospel
Read Acts 26:1-32

OUR TRIPS TO ISRAEL OFTEN BEGIN WITH A SURPRISE VISIT TO the sprawling, majestic seaport of Caesarea by the Sea, located on the beautiful coast of the Mediterranean and built by Herod the Great in honor of the Roman emperor. Herod the Great governed Judea from 37 to 4 B.C. and traded political favors with the Romans in order to maintain control over the Jews and insure peace in this turbulent part of the empire. It was a "scratch my back, and I'll scratch yours" arrangement for both Herod and the Romans.

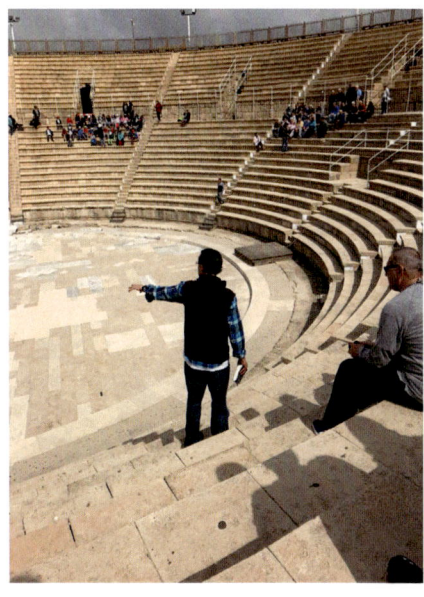

The neurotic and paranoid Herod ruled with an iron fist. In fact, he had one

of his wives and two of his sons killed for treason. One author wrote, "It was better to be Herod's dog than his son." Because Herod had access to Roman military might, he forced slaves to conduct a massive building campaign around the country, including this seaport city, which features the remains of a hippodrome, palace, and a great amphitheater still in use today.

Caesarea also is associated with four main characters whose stories intertwined with the Gospel: Pilate, Philip, Peter and Paul. In 1961, archaeologists discovered the famous "Pilate stone" at Caesarea, which provided the first extra-biblical reference to the Roman governor named, Pontius Pilate, who condemned Jesus to death.

Philip was commissioned by God to go to Gaza, met an Ethiopian treasurer on the way, and "told him the good news about Jesus" (Acts 8:35). After the treasurer was baptized and became one of the first Gentile converts, Philip returned to Caesarea.

Acts 10 describes how Peter received the vision of clean and unclean animals descending from heaven. God shattered Peter's prejudiced world view by commanding him to eat of both kinds of animals, symbolizing how all people deserve to hear the truth of the Gospel of Jesus Christ. With that image echoing in his thoughts, Peter received a commission from God to go to the house of Cornelius at Caesarea, the Roman centurion and God-fearing Gentile, who received Christ as a result of Peter's message.

Later, Scripture tells us that the Apostle Paul appeared before three different political characters: Felix, Festus, and King Agrippa II in Caesarea. In each case Paul testified to the power of the Gospel how "Christ would suffer and... rise from the dead..." (Acts 26:23).

Philip, Peter and Paul were missionaries of the Gospel – that Jesus died and rose from the dead so that God could offer forgiveness to all who believe in Him. The same is true for every follower of Jesus Christ. We are commissioned with the good news of the Gospel that transforms people from the kingdom of darkness to the kingdom of light and was proclaimed first to the Jew and also to the Gentile (Romans 1:16).

Today, you will encounter people who are far from God. Every co-worker, classmate, friend, relative, and neighbor is headed somewhere for eternity – in heaven with God or in hell apart from Him. Why not determine that you'll share that Good News every chance you get?

Prayer of reflection: Thank you, God, that somebody shared the Gospel with me. Would you help me today to see people through your eyes – headed to eternity with you in heaven or apart from you in hell?

My Prayer Journal

DAY 2

Beersheba

Theme: Trust & Obey
Read Hebrews 11:8-19

THE TEL OF BEERSHEBA IS LOCATED JUST A FEW KILOMETERS east of the modern city of Beersheba and provides a final stop before heading south into the Negev Desert. A tel is an artificial mound formed by one generation after another from the remains of rocks, mudbricks and other remnants from people who lived on the same site for thousands of years. It's impossible to visit this tel without discussing Abraham, the great patriarch and "friend of God." Even though he lived more than 4,000 years ago, the lessons from his life are just as relevant today.

If you're like me, you live by the motto, "Plan your work and work your plan." I have a "To Do" list every day that I use to accomplish projects and remind me of appointments. I doubt Abraham had much of a "To Do" list – except one thing: Obey God.

More than 4,000 years ago, the Lord told him, "Leave your native country, your relatives, and your father's family, and go to the land that I will show you" (Genesis 12:1 NLT). Imagine what it was like for Abraham to tell his mom and dad he was leaving his homeland, had no idea where he was going, and wanted them to go along?? Can you hear that conversation? "Where are you going??" "I don't know."

"Where will you live?" "I don't know." "Where will you work?" "I don't know." "Why are you leaving?" "God said to go." "But who is God?"

Scripture says, "It was by faith that Abraham obeyed when God called him to leave home and go to another land that God would give him as his inheritance. He went without knowing where he was going" (Hebrews 11:8 NLT). The result of Abraham's faith was obedience to God's direction – even though he had no idea where God was leading Him.

When I was a boy, we used to sing: "Trust and obey, for there's no other way, to be happy in Jesus, but to trust and obey." That really is the prescription for the kind of life God wants for every one of us. We trust God – then do what He says.

The Jews often repeat a comparable phrase: **"Do and listen."** In other words, do what God says, then figure out why He said it. That's what Abraham did. And that's a great prescription for life.

Prayer of reflection: Thank you, God, that you have a plan for my life. Help me to trust you and obey your direction – even when I don't have all the details.

My Prayer Journal

_____

_____

_____

_____

_____

_____

_____

_____

_____

_____

_____

_____

_____

_____

_____

_____

_____

_____

_____

_____

_____

_____

_____

DAY 3

Wilderness Tabernacle
At Timna

Theme: Sacrifice
Read Hebrews 9:24-28

PERHAPS NO BOOK IN THE BIBLE CAUSES MORE CONFUSION than Leviticus. Christians who have attempted to read through the Bible often get bogged down in the details of the sacrificial system described in this book. What's the difference between the guilt offering and the sin offering? What's the purpose of the Day of Atonement? Why were so many different sacrifices offered? Why were sacrifices even necessary? What does all this symbolize? A visit to the Wilderness Tabernacle at Timna helps answer these questions.

The Wilderness Tabernacle is located at the southern tip of the Negev, about 30 kilometers north of Eilat, and supplies a scale model of The Tabernacle detailed by God for His people in the Book of Exodus. This model contains replicas of the furniture used for the sacrificial system: the brazen altar, the copper washbasin, the golden menorah, the table of showbread, the priestly garments, and even the Ark of the Covenant. All are reminders that our perfect and holy God requires satisfaction because we have offended Him through our sin.

The writer of Hebrews describes how Jesus fully satisfied all that God requires in order for us to experience forgiveness for our sin. "And just as each person is destined to die once and after that comes judgment, so also Christ *was offered once for all time as a sacrifice* to take away the sins of many people. He will come again, not to deal with our sins, but to bring salvation to all who are eagerly waiting for him" (Hebrews 9:27-28 NLT).

Think of that! You don't need to pay for your own sin. Nothing else needs to be done. The sacrifice of Jesus is perfect and complete. Your forgiveness is assured when you trust what He has accomplished for you on Calvary. You can enjoy a relationship with God for eternity because of what Jesus accomplished through His death. Charles Wesley wrote: "Amazing love, how can it be? That Thou, My God, should die for me?"

Prayer of reflection: Lord, thank you for the forgiveness that Jesus offers me because of His death on the cross. Help me to demonstrate that same forgiveness to people I encounter today.

My Prayer Journal

DAY 4

The Land of Edom & Petra

Theme: Believe
Read Numbers 21:4-9

PETRA – JUST THE WORD CREATES A SENSE OF MYSTERY! MOST people who visit the Holy Land include a visit to this ancient city, built by the Nabateans in the 2nd Century B.C. A drive to Petra, "the red-rock city half as old as time" and one of the Seven New Wonders of the Ancient World, takes us through the Land of Edom in southern Jordan. During the Exodus from Egypt, the Israelites were not permitted by the Edomites to go through this land which would have been the shortest route.

God's people complained because of the hardships they endured in this desert. Frankly, it's a barren place, so it's not hard to imagine their grumbling! In summer – the temperatures are brutal! And the flies threaten to carry you away! All of this caused the Israelites to long for the land of Egypt. They griped against the Lord and His representative, Moses, so God brought judgment into their lives through venomous snakes.

At God's instruction, Moses created a bronze serpent and lifted it on a pole. As the people looked to that bronze serpent, they were healed of the life-threatening snake bites.

Jesus used that example to describe the power of His own crucifixion. "And as Moses lifted up the bronze snake on a pole in the wilderness, so the Son of Man must be lifted up, so that everyone who believes in him will have eternal life. For this

is how God loved the world: He gave his one and only Son, so that everyone who believes in him will not perish but have eternal life" (John 3:14-16 NLT).

What must we do to be saved? Acts 16:31 tells us, "Believe in the Lord Jesus, and you will be saved." Genuine belief can be summarized in the word, "trust." Just as we lean all of our weight on a chair when we sit down, so God invites us to lean all of our weight fully on Jesus to receive the forgiveness that He alone can provide through His death on Calvary.

Prayer of reflection: Lord Jesus, thank you that you endured death on a Roman cross just for me. Help me to trust you fully as the Only One who can secure my salvation for eternity.

My Prayer Journal

DAY 5

Mt. Nebo

Theme: Holiness
Read Deuteronomy 32:48-52

MOSES HAS OFTEN BEEN CALLED, "THE GREATEST LEADER OF Israel's history." Yet the Bible also describes him as "the meekest man in all the earth" (Numbers 12:3). He wasn't always like that.

During the first 40 years of his life, Moses probably thought he was something special. Rescued from the reeds of the Nile River as an infant, he lived a charmed life in the palace of the king of Egypt. One day, he saw an Egyptian beating a fellow-Israelite, so he intervened and killed the man.

He fled for his life and came to the land of Midian, where he spent the next 40 years caring for the flocks of his father-in-law. He learned survival skills in the desert, an invaluable asset which God would use during the last third of his life.

One day God called Moses from a burning bush and commissioned him to lead His people out of Egypt following 400 years of bondage. Moses then led the Israelites on the Exodus through the Sinai desert, across the dry land at the bottom of the Red Sea, through Midian, around Edom to the brink of the Promised Land. Along the

way God miraculously provided food and water for His people day after day.

On one occasion, Moses was commanded to speak to a rock so life-giving water could flow from it. Instead, because of his frustration with the griping of the Israelites, Moses struck the rock in anger. That one act of disobedience prevented Moses from entering the Promised Land (Numbers 20:12). That might sound harsh, but God was emphasizing for all of us, and for all-time, that He cannot tolerate sin.

His standard is not 99%. His standard is absolute perfection. Anything less cannot be tolerated.

Moses was prevented from experiencing the land of promise because he did not uphold God's holiness among the Israelites. (Deuteronomy 32:51).

Here's the question everyone should answer: How am I preventing God's blessing by my own disobedience? Is there some area of my life where God cannot pour out his blessings because I am not sensitive to Him?

Prayer of reflection: Lord God, what have I permitted in my life that is hindering the work you want to do in me and through me?

My Prayer Journal

DAY 6

Ein Gedi

Theme: Worship
Read Psalm 42:1-11

NOTHING IS QUITE AS REFRESHING AS A COOL DRINK ON A HOT summer day! Maybe that's one reason I love Ein Gedi so much. If you ever visit Israel in the summer, one thing is certain: the desert will be hot! Very hot! Like 110° hot!

Perhaps that's why Ein Gedi is so appealing. It's an oasis in the middle of the Judean desert. High in the hills, water gushes out of the rocks to form a beautiful stream with several waterfalls. This gorgeous, natural garden becomes the life-giving resource for vegetation and animals in the area. Ibex and hyrax often satisfy their thirst by the pools of Ein Gedi.

David knew this area like the back of his hand. In fact, it was like his playground... his backyard. He may have killed a lion and a bear in the area. When King Saul threatened David's life, the future king fled to the caves of Ein Gedi for safety.

One day, Saul came perilously close to capturing David. He went into one of the dozens of caves to "use the facilities," not knowing that David and his men were far back in the darkness. "David crept up unnoticed and cut off a corner of Saul's robe" (2 Samuel 24:4 NIV).

However, David was overcome with guilt because of his presumption. This tenderness to God's prodding became the hallmark of his life.

No wonder David was able to pen great psalms like: "Wash away all my iniquity and cleanse me from my sin. For I know my transgressions, and my sin is always before me. Cleanse me with hyssop and I will be clean; wash me, and I will be whiter than snow" (Psalms 51:2-3,7 NIV).

Above anything, David was a worshiper! With this backdrop in mind, he wrote, "As the deer pants for streams of water, so my soul pants for you, O God. My soul thirsts for God, for the living God. Where can I go and meet with God?" (Psalm 42:1-2 NIV).

David knew that the emptiness of life could only be satisfied by God himself. Pascal suggested that we have been created with a "God-shaped vacuum" that only He can fill.

Likewise, you and I were born to worship. We will worship something or someone, but we *will* worship. We might worship a job, a relationship, a hobby, a recreational pursuit, retirement, good health, or a thousand other things. We may not even realize what we worship – but we will worship.

Ein Gedi reminds us that only God can fill the void in our hearts to worship. 1600 years ago, Augustine wrote: "Thou hast made us for thyself, O Lord, and our heart is restless until it finds its rest in thee." So look at your life… Discover what you really worship. Realize that the emptiness in your heart will only be satisfied by the vitality of walking with the living God.

Prayer of reflection: Lord, would you show me the emptiness of filling my life with things that substitute for genuine worship of you?

My Prayer Journal

DAY 7

Qumran

Theme: Accuracy & Authority of the Word of God
Read 2 Timothy 3:14-17

DO YOU BELIEVE THE BIBLE IS THE WORD OF GOD? IF SO, WHY? After all, the Bible reminds us that "All Scripture is inspired by God" (2 Timothy 3:16 – NIV). How can we know that the Bible was originally "inspired by God?" A stop at Qumran helps clarify this issue.

In 1947 in a cave at Qumran of the Judean desert, a Jordanian shepherd boy stumbled on to what is arguably the greatest archaeological discovery of the 20th century – the Dead Sea Scrolls. He had no idea that the priceless clay pots of Qumran contained a wealth of evidence for the character of the Scriptures.

Before the Dead Sea Scrolls were uncovered, the oldest copies of the Old Testament, known

as Masoretic texts, dated about 1000 A.D. Jewish tradition says that scribes carefully hand-copied each book in the Hebrew Bible so that no mistakes were made. In fact, if a mistake was discovered in an ancient scroll, it would be discarded and destroyed. When scrolls became frayed and worn, they also were destroyed.

But how do we know the scribes did not edit those ancient documents to make them look as if they had supernatural origin? After all, in the Sixth Century B.C., Daniel prophesied about four great kingdoms that would eventually rule the world 1500 years before the Masoretic texts were compiled. How do we know that later scribes did not change the words of Daniel to make it look like he was actually writing prophecy about the Babylonians, Persians, Greeks, and Romans? It's one thing to describe accurately what has already happened in this world. That's history! It's something else entirely to  look ahead and accurately portray what will happen. That's prophecy!

When the Dead Sea Scrolls were analyzed, they dated about 200 years before the time of Christ. That's 1200 years earlier than those Masoretic texts! The clay pots of Qumran yielded fragments, even major sections, of every book in the Old Testament, except the story of Queen Esther. The scholars placed Dead Sea Scrolls and Masoretic texts side-by-side. What do you suppose they discovered? You could basically draw an equal sign (=) between them. There were no substantial differences that threatened the theology of the Old Testament text.

In other words, God not only inspired His Word, He preserved His Word for all of us. If the Bible is not accurate, it is not authoritative. The Dead Sea Scrolls remind us that the Word of God we hold in our hands is reliable. It's authentic. It can be trusted. "It is useful to teach us what is true and to make us realize what is wrong in our lives. It corrects us when we are wrong and teaches us to do what is right. God uses it to prepare and equip his people to do every good work" (2 Timothy 3:16-17 NLT).

Prayer of reflection: Father, help me to build my life around the accurate and authoritative teaching of the Word of God.

My Prayer Journal

DAY **8**

Bethany Beyond The Jordan

Theme: Magnify
Read John 3:23-30

WHO WAS THE LAST OF THE OLD TESTAMENT PROPHETS? WE could say it was John the Baptist. When he was asked about his identity, John replied in the words of the prophet Isaiah: "'I am a voice shouting in the wilderness, 'Clear the way for the Lord's coming!'" (John 1:23 NLT). Like many other Old Testament prophets, John's responsibility was to point people to the coming Messiah.

John's life was characterized by the eccentric, even the supernatural. His birth was announced by an angel to elderly and surprised parents. Because of his unbelief, Zacharias, his father, was unable to speak until he gave John his name at birth. John lived in the desert, wore clothes made of camel's hair and ate locusts and wild honey. His fiery messages proclaimed repentance and attracted great crowds to his ministry. He even baptized his followers in Bethany beyond the Jordan.

Finally, he came face-to-face with the Messiah and said, "Look! The Lamb of God who takes away the sin of the world!" (John 1:29 NLT). For the rest of his life, John had one primary message: "He must become greater and greater, and I must become less and less." (John 3:30 NLT). That should be the desire of every Christ-follower. The influence of Jesus in us should become greater and greater.

When he wrote to the Philippians, the Apostle Paul said, "…With all boldness, as always, so now also Christ shall be magnified in my body, whether it be by life, or by death. For to me to live is Christ, and to die is gain" (Philippians 1:20b-21 KJV). What does it mean to magnify something? It means to make it bigger! When people look at us – the character of Jesus should be more and more evident. They should see Him above anything else. Can you say that's the heartbeat of your life? It was for John!

Truth is … if we live to magnify the Lord Jesus, life may not be easy. It may be filled with challenges, hardships, even martyrdom. But there is no greater privilege in life than to magnify the Lord "whether by life or by death."

Prayer of reflection: Lord Jesus, would you be magnified in my life today so that people see more of you and less of me?

My Prayer Journal

DAY 9

Machaerus

Theme: Suffering
Read Matthew 14:1-12

ABOUT 100 YEARS BEFORE THE BIRTH OF CHRIST, A MOUNTAINTOP fortress known as Machaerus, was constructed over-looking the barren landscape of the eastern shore of the Dead Sea. It stands alone, like Alcatraz, as a reminder of the horrific events that occurred within its walls. Apparently, this fortress was utilized by Herod the Great, and eventually by his son, Herod Antipas.

The fortress is best known as the place of execution for John the Baptist. Antipas ordered John's murder because the courageous prophet had condemned him for his adulterous relationship with his brother's wife.

What did John do to deserve this kind of cruel punishment and death? After all, Jesus said this: "No one in history surpasses John…" (Matthew 11:11a MSG).

Apparently, John had the unique responsibility of "preparing the way for the Lord" (Matthew 3:1; John 1:23). That responsibility included boldly preaching the need for repentance in preparation for the coming Messiah – even to the king of the country. And that cost him his life!

One of the paradoxes of the Christian life is that God will ask some of His faithful followers to go through times of great pain and suffering – all for the sake of the Gospel. That was true for the greatest missionary who ever lived: The Apostle Paul. He wrote: "I have worked much harder, been in prison more frequently, been flogged more severely, and been exposed to death again and again. Five times I received from the Jews the forty lashes minus one. Three times I was beaten with rods, once I was pelted with stones, three times I was shipwrecked, I spent a night and a day in the open sea, I have been constantly on the move. I have been in danger from rivers, in danger from bandits, in danger from my fellow Jews, in danger from Gentiles; in danger in the city, in danger in the country, in danger at sea; and in danger from false believers. I have labored and toiled and have often gone without sleep; I have known hunger and thirst and have often gone without food; I have been cold and naked. Besides everything else, I face daily the pressure of my concern for all the churches" (2 Corinthians 11:23b-28 NIV).

Over the years, I have watched godly people suffer and even die. I have stood in their presence as they breathed their last breath … and marveled at their radiant testimony for Jesus. It feels like a holy moment as a child of God slips from this life to the next.

Perhaps you, too, are facing adversity, pain, even death. Could I just remind you of the privilege you have to reflect the character of Christ in your life – even in times of hardship? Paul, who knew so much about suffering, wrote: "For you have been given not only the privilege of trusting in Christ but also the privilege of suffering for him." (Philippians 1:29 NLT)

Prayer of reflection: Heavenly Father, would you help me to see the hardships and suffering of my life as a privilege to point others to you?

My Prayer Journal

DAY 10

Bethlehem – The Shepherds' Fields

Theme: The Incarnation
Read Luke 2:1-14

BETHLEHEM TODAY LOOKS NOTHING LIKE IT DID AT THE BIRTH of Jesus. The sprawling city of 40,000 people is filled with street vendors, souvenir shops, tourist buses – even a mall. Obviously, Joseph and Mary had none of those conveniences when they made that long trek from Nazareth.

Today, the Church of the Nativity stands over a series of caves that may have been the location where our Lord entered this world. But as is often the case in the Holy Land, the decorations of a church building obscure the surroundings for a supernatural event described in Scripture.

That's the case in Bethlehem. So it's helpful to make our way out of town to the Shepherds' Fields. There, it's not hard to imagine the account recorded by Dr. Luke, which has become some of the most famous words in the Bible:

"And Joseph also went up from Galilee, out of the city of Nazareth, into Judaea, unto the city of David, which is called Bethlehem;

(because he was of the house and lineage of David:) To be taxed with Mary his espoused wife, being great with child. And so it was, that, while they were there, the days were accomplished that she should be delivered. And she brought forth her firstborn son, and wrapped him in swaddling clothes, and laid him in a manger; because there was no room for them in the inn" (Luke 2:4-7 KJV).

Think about the glory of those words! The Son of God, the Creator of the universe, took a human body to identify with us. We call that "the incarnation." The word means "in flesh." John says, "The Word became human and made his home among us" (John 1:14a NLT).

Here's the question all of us should ponder: Why would Jesus come to this earth? Why would He "make his home among us?" There's only one answer: He wants us to get to know Him. As God in a human body, He revealed what God is like.

The Apostle Paul probably quoted the actual words of early believers when he wrote: "Without question, this is the great mystery of our faith: Christ was revealed in a human body...." (1 Timothy 3:16 NLT). The Apostle John continues, "He was full of unfailing love and faithfulness. And we have seen his glory, the glory of the Father's one and only Son" (John 1:14b NLT).

Prayer of reflection: Lord Jesus, thank you that you came to earth so I could know you. Help me to comprehend today more of who you are and what you have done for me.

My Prayer Journal

DAY 11

Bethlehem – The Herodian

Theme: Humility
Read Philippians 2:1-11

No question about it... Herod the Great loved the good life! The remains of more than ten of his palaces dot the landscape throughout Israel. Nothing demonstrates more his madness and quest for glory than the Herodian. It's a majestic man-made mountain that rises 2,457 feet above sea level – the highest point in the Judean desert.

Herod thought he knew where he wanted to spend eternity... at the Herodian. So he prepared his own tomb on the mountain. In *Wars of the Jews*, Flavius Josephus, the first century historian, describes the funeral of Herod with these words: He "omitted nothing of magnificence. . . there was a bier all of gold, embroidered with precious stones, and a purple bed of various contexture, with the dead body upon it, covered with purple; and a diadem was put upon his head, and a crown of gold above it . . the body was carried two hundred furlongs, to Herodian, where he had given order to be buried."

That was typical of Herod. Even in his death, he longed for the opulence and grandeur that came to a king.

What a contrast with Jesus! As the King of kings, He enjoyed the worship of the angels before His birth in Bethlehem. But He willingly surrendered the grandeur of heaven to identify with us and accomplish the purpose of His Father here on earth.

Paul wrote: "…He gave up his divine privileges; he took the humble position of a slave and was born as a human being. When he appeared in human form, he humbled himself in obedience to God and died a criminal's death on a cross" (Philippians 2:7-8 NLT).

Again, we ask why? Why would Jesus surrender all that grandeur for the most humble life imaginable? Here's the answer: "You know the generous grace of our Lord Jesus Christ. Though he was rich, yet for your sakes he became poor, so that by his poverty he could make you rich" (2 Corinthians 8:9 – NLT).

King Herod wanted glory for himself, so he erected a majestic palace at the Herodian where he could command the adoration of his subjects. Jesus, the Son of God, was born right under Herod's nose in a cave of Bethlehem in the most humble circumstance. One king forced his subjects into poverty while he became rich. The other King became poor so that we might experience the riches of heaven for all eternity with Him.

Prayer of reflection: Lord Jesus, thank you for surrendering the worship of the angels so that I could enjoy the glory of heaven forever.

My Prayer Journal

DAY 12

Nazareth

Theme: Rejection
Read Luke 4:14-30

WHEN I WAS IN SCHOOL, MY CLASSMATES OFTEN CALLED ME a particular nickname. I hated it. Every time I heard that name, it reminded me I wasn't in the popular crowd. Today, we would probably call that bullying.

No matter what name you give it, nobody likes to be rejected. But nothing is more painful than to be rejected by your own family and friends. That happened to Jesus.

Early in his ministry, he went to Nazareth, entered the synagogue, and began to read from the scroll of Isaiah: "The Spirit of the Lord is on me, because he has anointed me to preach good news to the poor, he has sent me to proclaim

freedom for the prisoners and recovery of sight for the blind, to release the oppressed, to proclaim the year of the Lord's favor" (Luke 4:18-19 NIV).

The eyes of everyone were glued on him as he read those words. They recognized those words to be a messianic prophecy. And then Jesus confirmed it: "Today this scripture is fulfilled in your hearing" (Luke 4:21 – NIV).

"Could it be?" they must have thought. "Is it possible that this son of Joseph, the stoneworker, is the Political Deliverer who will free us from the hated Romans and restore the glory of the kingdom to Israel?"

Then Jesus did the unthinkable for a Jewish rabbi. He turned the attention of his biased audience to the hated Gentiles around them. He reminded them that Elijah was sent to a Gentile widow in a community not far away and that Naaman, the Syrian, was the only leper healed during the days of Elisha.

The reaction of the citizens of Nazareth was predictable! No self-respecting rabbi would show compassion to the Gentiles. But Jesus did! So they "drove him out of the town, and took him to the brow of the hill on which the town was built, in order to throw him down the cliff. But he walked right through the crowd and went on his way" (Luke 4:29-30 NIV).

Perhaps you've been ridiculed and mocked for doing what is right. Perhaps those who know you have turned against you. Perhaps you've never even known the love of a family.

If you've ever felt rejection, take heart. Jesus knows how you feel. You are in great company! The Apostle John wrote: "He came to his own people, and even they rejected him. But to all who believed him and accepted him, he gave the right to become children of God" (John 1:11-12 NLT).

Prayer of reflection: Jesus, thank you that you understand how it feels to be rejected. Thank you for loving me, even when I'm not lovable.

My Prayer Journal

DAY 13

Capernaum

Theme: Sensitivity to God
Read Matthew 11:20-24

My wife and I have been blessed with an amazing spiritual heritage. Our parents demonstrated what it means to walk with God. Both our paternal and maternal grandparents knew the Lord. All of these family members prayed for us from the time we were born. We owe all of them an eternal debt of gratitude.

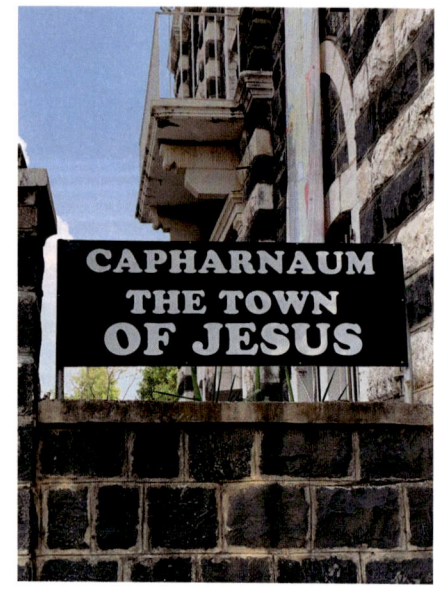

Both of our fathers traveled from coast to coast, and to other countries of the world, to present the message of hope in Jesus Christ to people who are far from God. For more than 60 years, I have met people who began a relationship with Jesus because of my own dad's influence in their lives.

Do you know the danger of that heritage? It's the danger of familiarity. Have you heard the old saying, "Familiarity breeds contempt?" It's possible for that to happen with the things of God. Many who have been raised in Christian homes and gone to church most of their lives have discovered that "Jesus" is the answer for almost every question that is asked. That's why it's easy to become too familiar with the things of God.

For three years the people of Jesus' hometown saw him perform miracles and heard him provide meaningful insights about life. Yet Jesus said, "You people of Capernaum, will you be honored in heaven? No, you will go down to the place of the dead. For, if the miracles I did for you had been done in wicked Sodom, it would still be here today. I tell you, even Sodom will be better off on judgment day than you" (Matthew 11:23-24 NLT).

There's a strong warning about becoming insensitive to the things of God: "We must pay the most careful attention, therefore, to what we have heard, so that we do not drift away" (Hebrews 2:1 NIV). "Do you show contempt for the riches of his kindness, forbearance and patience, not realizing that God's kindness is intended to lead you to repentance?" (Romans 2:4 NIV)

Familiarity doesn't have to breed contempt or apathy. It can breed worship! The more we walk with God, the more sensitive we should become to the things of God.

So, if you have been blessed with a godly heritage, take a moment to thank God for all that He has provided for you. Begin to list all of the ways He has blessed your life and provided for your good. That's a wonderful gift! So don't take it for granted, and don't fall prey to the trap of familiarity.

Prayer of reflection: Holy Spirit, would you produce in me a new love for Jesus and an appreciation for the heritage you have given me?

My Prayer Journal

_____

_____

_____

_____

_____

_____

_____

_____

_____

_____

_____

_____

_____

_____

_____

_____

_____

_____

_____

_____

_____

_____

_____

Boat Ride on The Sea of Galilee

Theme: Faith, Hope, and Love
Read Mark 6:45-56

A VISIT TO THE SEA OF GALILEE ENABLES US TO UNDERSTAND why Jesus loved this area. He called 11 of his 12 disciples from this region. Many were prosper-

ous fishermen. It's a serene setting. The tranquility of the lake
provides a quiet contrast to
the hustle and bustle of cities
like Jerusalem.

But the lake is not always
calm. It has the ability to surprise
even experienced fishermen.
That happened on more than one
occasion with the disciples of
the Lord.

After a long day of minis-
try, Jesus sent his disciples to the

other side of the lake to teach them about *faith*. "The disciples were in trouble far away from land, for a strong wind had risen, and they were fighting heavy waves. About three o'clock in the morning Jesus came toward them, walking on the water. When the disciples saw him walking on the water, they were terrified. In their fear, they cried out, 'It's a ghost!' But Jesus spoke to them at once. "Don't be afraid," he said. "Take courage. I am here!" (Matthew 14:24-27 NLT).

Nothing brings greater courage in the middle of the storms of life than to recognize the One who said, "Never will I leave you; never will I forsake you" (Hebrews 13:5 NLT).

A few moments later, "Peter called to him, 'Lord, if it's really you, tell me to come to you, walking on the water.' 'Yes, come,' Jesus said.

So Peter went over the side of the boat and *began to walk on the water* toward Jesus! "But when he saw the strong wind and the waves, he was terrified and began to sink. 'Save me, Lord!' he shouted. Jesus immediately reached out and grabbed him. 'You have so little faith,' Jesus said. 'Why did you doubt me?' When they climbed back into the boat, the wind stopped" (Matthew 14:28-32 NLT).

Have you ever felt like you were about to "go under" for the last time in life? It's easy to feel hopeless in that moment. Yet here Jesus reminded Peter and the rest of the disciples that *hope* comes in the trials of life when we grab the hand of the Master.

Later, after his resurrection, Jesus went back to this tranquil place and taught his disciples about *love*. Three times, Jesus asked Peter, "Do you love me?" Peter must have doubted his own ability to answer any question following his earlier denial of the Lord.

In these three moments, Jesus reminded us of what Paul would later write to the Corinthians: "And now these three remain: faith, hope and love. But the greatest of these is love" (1 Corinthians 13:13).

Prayer of reflection: Thank you, Jesus, that you embodied these three great qualities while you were on earth. Would you develop these attributes in me today?

My Prayer Journal

DAY 15

Caesarea Philippi

Theme: The Church
Read Matthew 16:13-20

A VISIT TO CAESAREA PHILIPPI HELPS US UNDERSTAND WHY Jesus was the Master Teacher. This city provides a magnificent view of sheer rock at the base of Mount Hermon. Ancient people believed that the impressive cave in that sheer rock face was the entrance to the underworld. In their view, the cave led to hell itself.

With that impressive backdrop, Jesus asked a penetrating question, "Who do men say that I am?" Peter, who so often failed, clearly passed this test when he answered, "You are the Christ, the Son of the Living God" (Matthew 16:18 NASB).

Then Jesus uttered these fascinating words: "Now I say to you that you are Peter (which means 'rock'), and upon this rock I will build my church, and all the powers of hell will not conquer it." (Matthew 16:18 NLT).

What is the "rock" on which Jesus promised to build His church? Was it Peter himself? No, otherwise Jesus would have said something like, "You are Peter, and because you are a rock, I will build my church on you." But he didn't say that.

Jesus used the meaning of Peter's name as a teaching tool. Jesus didn't promise to build His church on Peter or his name. He promised

to build His church on Peter's great declaration that Jesus is the "Christ, the Son of the living God." That is the foundation on which the Church of Jesus Christ rests! That is theological bedrock! If you want to be a part of God's Church, you must accept the idea that Jesus is The Promised One, The Messiah, God Incarnate.

But there's more... Jesus said that "The powers of hell will not conquer it" (Matthew 16:18b NLT). I wonder if Jesus looked straight into that cave, thought in His day to be the entrance of hell, when He made that bold statement.

Think about that when you are discouraged, defeated, or depressed. If you believe that "Jesus is the Christ, the Son of the living God," you are part of the Church. And all the forces of Evil will not defeat the Church!

You don't need to cower in fear. You don't need to worry or fret. You are on the winning side. You can experience victory because Jesus, the Lord of the Church, has promised nothing less.

Prayer of reflection: Thank you, Lord Jesus, that the Church is your idea and that you have invited me to be a part of it.

My Prayer Journal

DAY 16

The Dead Sea

Theme: Serving
Read Romans 12:3-8

IT'S ONE OF THE MOST FASCINATING SPOTS ON EARTH. IT ALSO happens to be the lowest place you can step on this planet. The Dead Sea rests more than 1300 feet below sea level. Springs at the base of Mt Hermon in Upper Galilee supply water for the Jordan River which empties into this catch-basin more than 100 miles south.

No question about it… it's dead! I've never seen a fisherman along its banks or a fishing boat with a large catch. More than a dozen minerals like magnesium, potassium, and calcium are mined from its waters. But nothing lives there!!

What causes all that dead-ness?? The Dead Sea has no outlet. Water flows in but does not flow out.

Oh, it looks beautiful – especially to a thirsty hiker who has walked the hot trails of the Judean desert. But you won't find a refreshing drink here! In fact, if you try to float in the Dead Sea, don't get the water in your eyes or mouth! It's painful!!

What a valuable lesson for every Christ-follower! The Apostle Peter wrote: "Each of you should use whatever gift you have received to serve others…." (1 Peter 4:10a NIV). God has sovereignly given His

children gifts *to use* to honor Him and help others. When we refuse to use what God has given us, we become like the Dead Sea … all intake and no outflow. In fact, others find it painful to be with us because we are so self-centered.

No wonder Jesus called us to a life of service! He even said, "… Whoever wants to become great among you must be your servant" (Matthew 20:26b NIV). So think about how you "taste" to others today. Are you bitter and self-centered – even painful to be around? Or are you a "breath of fresh air"– even life-giving – because you use what God has given you to bless others?

Prayer of reflection: Father, thank you for the gifts You have given me. Would You empower me to use those for Your glory and the good of others?

My Prayer Journal

DAY 17

Magdala

Theme: Freedom
Read Romans 7:15-25

SOMETIMES IT SEEMS LIKE EVERY SHOVELFUL OF DIRT IN ISRAEL reveals a fascinating historical discovery. That happened in Magdala a few years ago.

Land was purchased by a priest along the Western shore of the Sea of Galilee in order to build a guesthouse for pilgrims who traveled to the Holy Land. Before construction could begin, the required excavations were conducted in 2009 by the Israeli Antiquities Authority.

Then it happened! Archaeologists stumbled upon the ancient fishing village of Magdala, perhaps the most prominent town along the shores of the Sea of Galilee in the first century. Along with the remnants of this fishing village, a first century synagogue was unearthed, only one of seven in the world left from that time. It's thrilling to walk through the ruins of this location and realize that Jesus walked the same steps.

Archaeologists also uncovered the "Magdala stone," which includes a carving of a seven-branch menorah. This kind of menorah can only be seen here and on the Arch of Titus in Rome. Whoever carved one menorah probably also carved the other based on a personal observation of the Temple in Jerusalem.

Many Bible scholars believe that Mary Magdalene hailed from this prominent fishing village. In fact we read this account from Dr. Luke: "Soon afterward Jesus began a tour of the nearby towns and villages, preaching and announcing the Good News about the Kingdom of God. He took his twelve disciples with him, along with some women who had been cured of evil spirits and diseases. Among them were Mary Magdalene, from whom he had cast out seven demons…." (Luke 8:1-2 – NLT).

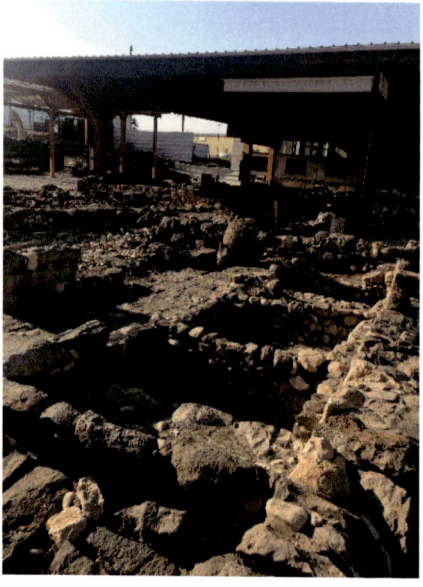

Mary had experienced the horrors of a life characterized by demon possession.

In fact, some believe that Mary's demonic influence led her into prostitution, but there is no biblical confirmation of that idea. We do know that Jesus freed her from spiritual bondage, as he did many others (Luke 7:21; 8:36), so she became a devoted follower and financial supporter of the Lord.

In fact, Mary's devotion to Jesus brought her to the tomb to anoint His body on that first Easter morning. She was among the first to hear the earth-shattering words of the angel: "He is not here; he has risen, just as he said" (Matthew 28:6 – NIV).

Do you feel like you are battling a habit that you cannot break? Perhaps you succumb to an addictive behavior. Maybe you feel bound by guilt and shame. Here's the great news... The same Jesus who delivered Mary from demon possession can deliver you from your spiritual bondage. Your chains can be broken by the power of the Resurrected Lord!

The Apostle Paul wrote these words to the Romans: "Oh, what a miserable person I am! Who will free me from this life that is dominated by sin and death? Thank God! The answer is in Jesus Christ our Lord" (Romans 7:24-25a – NLT).

Prayer of Reflection: Almighty God, help me to tap Your infinite power and wisdom today to break the chains of spiritual bondage that keep me from experiencing the life You designed for me.

My Prayer Journal

DAY 18

Tel Aviv

Theme: Rest
Read Hebrews 4:1-12

SEVERAL YEARS AGO, I WAS INVITED TO JOIN OTHER EVANGELICAL leaders at a Jewish home for an evening meal on Shabbat. It's an experience I won't forget. The entire family gathered around the table for a wonderful dinner. Throughout the evening, prayers were recited, blessings given, and Scripture read.

Shabbat begins about sundown on Friday evening and concludes near sundown on Saturday evening. A very careful schedule is distributed to observant Jewish families containing exact minutes when Shabbat begins and ends, as well as other important observances during that 24-hour period. The purpose of Shabbat is, of course, to follow the command of the Lord who said, "Remember the Sabbath day by keeping it holy."

Truth is, many who claim a Jewish heritage do not observe Shabbat. I have been in Tel Aviv on Friday evening, and it's party time for many Israelis! Restaurants and bars are open late as non-observant Jews enjoy their weekend. The beach is usually packed on warm Saturdays with locals just enjoying the sand, surf, and sun.

Frankly, this principle has always been an enigma to me. I never liked "taking a nap" as a boy. It's the one command out of the 10 Commandments that is not repeated for Christians in the New Testament, so I probably ignored the value of a Sabbath many times in my life.

Yet the principle of observing a day of rest with your family seems like a valuable idea, even under the New Covenant. After all, God said, "You have six days each week for your ordinary work. For in six days the Lord made the heavens, the earth, the sea, and everything in them; but on the seventh day he rested. That is why the Lord blessed the Sabbath day and set it apart as holy" (Exodus 20:9,11 NLT). Apparently, the Lord Jesus recognized the value of this principle: "Jesus often withdrew to the wilderness for prayer" (Luke 5:16 NLT).

Now I'm not suggesting you have to keep a Sabbath on a certain day or in a certain way. Paul even wrote to the Colossians: "So don't let anyone condemn you for what you eat or drink, or for not celebrating certain holy days or new moon ceremonies or Sabbaths" (Colossians 2:16 NLT).

Just figure out how you can "rest from your work" one day of the week and take time on that day to especially honor the Lord. You might become more productive in your work. And you just might like it!

Prayer of reflection: Father, thank you for setting the example for me to rest. Help me this week to find time to rest from my work and worship You.

My Prayer Journal

The Western Wall

Theme: Prayer
Read Matthew 7:7-11

SEVERAL YEARS AGO, WHEN I VISITED THE WESTERN WALL, I heard something that I had never noticed. As parents brought their small children, I heard boys and girls saying, "Abba Abba!" Do you know what that means? It means "daddy!" It's the most personal name for a human father that a child could say.

Now Paul wrote to the Galatians: *"...God has sent forth the Spirit of His Son into our hearts, crying, 'Abba! Father!'" (Galatians 4:6 NASB).* Think about that! When we pray, it's a *personal conversation with the Father in heaven who loves to give good gifts to His kids.*

But without a personal relationship with the Father, our

prayers will be powerless and ineffective. So how do we develop a per-sonal relationship with God? Jesus answered that question!! He said, "No one comes to the Father except through me…" (John 14:6b NIV). Apart from Jesus, we lack a relationship with the Father in Heaven because of our own sin and self-centeredness.

When Jesus died on that Roman cross 2,000 years ago and came back to life at His resurrection - God the Father provided the way for us to experience His forgiveness for all of our sin and have that relationship with Him right now. Paul wrote that Jesus "made peace for us with God through the blood of his cross…" (Col. 1:15 NIV).

However, we must *choose that relationship by faith* in what he's done for us. Without faith - it's impossible to please God! And once we begin this relationship with Jesus Christ, it's possible for us to have this personal conversation with God the Father at any time!

I love these words of J. I. Packer in his great work, *Knowing God*: "*Knowing God is more than knowing about him; it's a matter of*

dealing with him as he opens up to you, and being dealt with by him....
Friends... Open their hearts to each other by what they say and do..."

Now here's the thing... This personal conversation is all based on what Jesus has done for us. That's why Jesus said: "I will do whatever you ask in my name, so that the Father may be glorified in the Son" (John 14:13 NIV).

When you think about it... It's almost absurd to think that The All-Powerful God of this Universe is going to alter things in answer to prayer. *But that is exactly what Jesus said He will do!*

Years ago, the great missionary, Hudson Taylor wrote, *"When we work, we work; but when we pray, God works."* Everything we do that's worth doing, everything God wants to do in your church, everything God wants to do in your home, and everything God wants to do in your life, He has subjugated to one thing: prayer!

Prayer of Reflection: Father, thank you so much for all that you offer me through the work of Jesus, your Son. May I view prayer as a personal conversation with my Loving Father who loves to give me just what I need.

My Prayer Journal

DAY 20

The Holocaust Museum

Theme: Depravity
Read Romans 3:10-26

A VISIT TO ISRAEL IS INCOMPLETE WITHOUT A TOUR OF THE Holocaust Museum, called Yad Vashem. The museum depicts the rise and fall of Nazi Germany throughout Europe during World War II.

During those days Hitler and his henchmen directed their hatred against God's people, the Jews. Cities like Dachau, Birkenbau and Treblinka will be forever linked with the heartache, slaughter and agony of the Jews. More than 6 million Jews were murdered during those horrific days, including 1 million children.

As you walk the halls of the museum, you see photos, letters, maps, and videos which all describe the agony of those moments. It's hard to leave without being depressed because of the tragic events portrayed within those walls.

Many times, visitors are tempted to ask, "How could anyone do this? What did the Jews do to deserve this? What could anyone do to deserve this kind of treatment?" There is only one answer: The depravity of the human heart breeds this kind of hatred.

The Apostle Paul paints this graphic picture in Romans: "All have turned away, they have together become worthless; there is no one who

does good, not even one. There is no fear of God before their eyes. For all have sinned and fall short of the glory of God." (Romans 3:12,18, 23 NIV).

We are all born rebels. I was born that way. So were you. You don't have to teach a two-year-old to stand defiantly before a 200-pound adult and say, "No!" It comes naturally! Jeremiah wrote that "The heart is deceitful and desperately wicked. Who can know it?" (Jeremiah 17:9 NIV).

Apart from the limitless mercy and grace of God, every one of us is capable of the most heinous crimes! But God in His mercy offers help. He alone offers to justify us "freely by his grace through the redemption that came by Christ Jesus" (Romans 3:24 NIV).

Whatever you may have done in your past... Whatever pain you might have created for others and for yourself... No matter how hopeless your life might seem... There is hope in Jesus. You can be forgiven! When you place your faith in what Jesus has done for you through his death on the cross, you can experience a new life and become a trophy of His love for you.

Prayer of reflection: Father, help me to identify the dark places in my own life that create havoc for me and those around me. I claim Your forgiveness based on Your mercy and grace available through Christ.

My Prayer Journal

DAY 21

Megiddo

Theme: Victory
Read Revelation 16:1-21

I'VE LIVED NEAR CLEVELAND FOR OVER 40 YEARS. I WILL NEVER forget the celebration in the summer of 2016 after the Cavaliers won the NBA championship – Cleveland's first professional sports championship in more than 50 years. More than 1 million people attended the mid-summer parade and party to honor that team. Do you know why? Everybody loves a winner!

No one wants to be on the losing side – especially for eternity! That principle is crystal clear when you stand on top of the Tel of Megiddo and look down on the Jezreel Valley. This magnificent plain, roughly 150 square miles, stretches nearly from the shores of the Mediterranean to the Jordan Valley. It's rich in agriculture and history. Generals have viewed this majestic basin as a perfect battlefield. British General Edmund Allenby defeated the Turks here at the end of World War I.

Scripture says there is coming a day when the Forces of Evil will join together in this valley for "battle against the Lord on that great judgment day of God the Almighty" (Revelation 16:14 NLT). It is a time when "all the nations (are gathered) to fight against Jerusalem" (Zechariah 14:2 NASB).

Do you know where these armies join as one against the Lord? The Apostle John answers: "Then they gathered the Kings together to the place that in Hebrew is called Armageddon" (Revelation 16:16 NIV). Hell is unleashed on the earth like never before.

For a while, things appear hopeless for the children of Israel and the Forces of Good. Suddenly Jesus appears in power and glory. "His eyes are like blazing fire, and on his head are many crowns. He has a name written on him that no one knows but he himself. He is dressed in a robe dipped in blood, and his name is the word of God. The armies of heaven were following him... out of his mouth comes a sharp sword with which to strike down the nations.... On his robe and on his thigh he has this name written: king of kings and Lord of lords" (Revelation 19:12-16 NIV).

This is a quick battle! There is no overtime. Jesus is joined by the "the armies of heaven" and swiftly defeats the Forces of Evil led by the Antichrist. Talk about ultimate victory!

So whatever you're facing, remember, if you're a child of God, you are on the winning team. You will not lose life's last battle. Victory is secure. You don't need to fear what's ahead because someday you will experience the glorious victory that Jesus alone delivers as King of kings and Lord of lords.

Prayer of reflection: Thank you, Almighty God, that You are ultimately in control on this earth. Help me to live victoriously in Your strength anticipating that day when You will rule and reign.

My Prayer Journal

_____

_____

_____

_____

_____

_____

_____

_____

_____

_____

_____

_____

_____

_____

_____

_____

_____

_____

_____

_____

_____

_____

_____

DAY 22

The Mount of Olives

Theme: Passion & Prophecy
Read Zechariah 14: 2-11

THE VIEW FROM THE MOUNT OF OLIVES PROVIDES A magnificent panorama of the Temple Mount and the Old City of Jerusalem. From the western slopes of this beautiful hillside, it's easy to imagine the trail Jesus followed on that first Palm Sunday as He rode into Jerusalem on the foal of a donkey to the cries of "Blessed is the king who comes in the name of the Lord! Peace in heaven and glory in the highest!" (Luke 19:38 NIV). This event introduced the last week before our Lord was crucified, often called, "Passion Week."

As you walk down the mountain, you can also gaze

across the Kidron Valley and see the only gate in the walls of the Old City that is closed – the Eastern or Golden Gate. It has been sealed because it's located just above a Muslim cemetery.

In AD 1540, the Eastern Gate was shut by order of Suleiman the Magnificent, who also rebuilt many of the current walls around the

Old City. Many suggest that the Gate was closed to prevent the Messiah from entering since Jewish tradition suggests that the Messiah will pass through the Eastern Gate when He comes to rule. Therefore, the Eastern Gate has remained sealed for almost 500 years.

This prominent mountain, therefore, also serves as a focal point for Bible prophecy. The Bible says that Jerusalem will become a target for all the nations of the world in the future. Yet God protects His people. "On that day the Lord will shield those who live in Jerusalem, so that the feeblest among them will be like David, and the house of David will be like God, like the angel of the Lord going before them. On that day I will set out to destroy all the nations that attack Jerusalem" (Zechariah 12:8-9 NIV).

Zechariah describes how the Messiah settles the score on Jerusalem: "Then the Lord will go out to fight against those nations, as he has fought in times past. On that day his feet will stand on the Mount of Olives, east of Jerusalem. And the Mount of Olives will split apart, making a wide valley running from east to west. Half the mountain will move toward the north and half toward the south" (Zechariah 14:3-4 NLT).

This graphic scene unfolds right on the Mount of Olives! Imagine the cosmic upheaval that occurs because the Son of God comes in justice to rule and reign on this earth. The world has never experienced anything like it!

Prayer of reflection: Despite the global uncertainties today, thank you, Lord, that You will someday reign and create a time of great peace for this world.

My Prayer Journal

DAY 23

GETHSEMANE

Theme: Agony
Read Matthew 26:36-47

DESCEND FROM THE MOUNT OF OLIVES, AND YOU DISCOVER a peaceful garden called Gethsemane amidst crowded streets filled with tourist buses, vendors, and pedestrians. Next to the Garden of Eden, it may be the most famous garden in the Bible. Even today, groups with a reservation can gather for reflection and prayer in a private section across an alley to contemplate what happened here the night before Jesus died.

The word Gethsemane means, "oil press." It's not surprising that a grove of olive trees still stands nearby today. It's even possible to

walk about 100 yards to visit a cave where Jesus likely spent His last hours with His disciples.

Matthew describes those hours with these words: "Then Jesus went with his disciples to a place called Gethsemane, and he said to them, 'Sit here while I go over there and pray.' He took Peter and the two sons of

Zebedee along with him, and he began to be sorrowful and troubled. Then he said to them, 'My soul is overwhelmed with sorrow to the point of death. Stay here and keep watch with me.' Going a little farther, he fell with his face to the ground and prayed, 'My Father, if it is possible, may this cup be taken from me. Yet not as I will, but as you will.' Then he returned to his disciples and found them sleeping. 'Couldn't you men keep watch with me for one hour?' he asked Peter. 'Watch and pray so that you will not fall into temptation. The spirit is willing, but the flesh is weak'" (Matthew 26:36-41 NIV). This scenario is repeated twice more in Gethsemane before Judas comes to betray the Lord.

No one can fully understand the agony of the Lord during those hours. It's ironic that Jesus wrestled with the Father's will in that location since Gethsemane implies the idea of "pressing." The Bible even says He "sweat great drops of blood" as He contemplated the horrors of the cross.

What caused this great anguish for the Lord? Was it just the thought of crucifixion on a Roman cross? No. As horrific as that would be, it was the idea that, for the only time in eternity past, present or future, God the Father and God the Son would be separated.

Jesus boldly proclaimed the eternal unity of the Godhead with statements like these: "I and the Father are one" (John 10:30 NIV). "That they may be one as we are one— I in them and you in me—so that they may be brought to complete unity" (John 17:22b NIV).

In Gethsemane, Jesus wrestled with the fracture of that relationship because He would bear the penalty for our sins in His body. The Apostle Paul summarizes the Lord's motivation in Gethsemane: "God made him who had no sin to be sin for us, so that in him we might become the righteousness of God" (2 Corinthians 5:21 NIV). What Jesus accomplished for us on the cross enables us to experience the perfect righteousness of God credited to our spiritual bank account! That's an offer too good to refuse.

Prayer of reflection: Thank you, Jesus, that you were willing to face the agony of the cross so that I could be made right with a holy God for all eternity.

My Prayer Journal

_____

_____

_____

_____

_____

_____

_____

_____

_____

_____

_____

_____

_____

_____

_____

_____

_____

_____

_____

_____

_____

_____

Beneath Calvary in The Church of The Holy Sepulcher

Theme: Mercy & Grace
Read Ephesians 2:1-10

OF ALL THE PLACES WE VISIT ON A TRIP TO THE HOLY LAND, this is my favorite. It lies deep within the Church of the Holy Sepulcher in a cave, at bedrock, and beneath the traditional location for Calvary.

Most tour groups don't go anywhere near the spot. But I like to bring groups here, or come alone. There's nothing glamorous about it.

Many stand in long lines for small chapels within the Church just to see the traditional locations of the crucifixion and resurrection of our Lord. Some people kiss the stones which mark those spots. Others fall on their faces and lie on the ground in an act of reverence. These places evoke such deep emotions for those who visit.

I prefer to walk down a few dozen steps to what feels like the basement of the church. Instead of frightful memories about dark church

basements I experienced as a boy, great words of an old song always flood my mind in that ancient cave. "Mercy there was great and grace was free. Pardon there was multiplied to me. There my burdened soul found liberty – at Calvary." This place always brings me to tears. All that is true because of the cross!

"Mercy is great!" God does not give us what we deserve. That's mercy. We deserve His justice and condemnation. Instead – He gives us repeated opportunities to respond to His offer of forgiveness. Titus 3:5 declares: "Not by works of righteousness which we have done but according to His mercy, He saved us …." (Titus 3:5 NIV).

"And grace was free!" As someone said, "It might be free, but it's not cheap." It cost Jesus His life! Because of the death of Jesus, God gives us what we don't deserve – eternity in heaven with Him. Paul wrote to the Ephesians: "It is by grace through faith we have been saved" (Ephesians 2:8).

Another songwriter penned: "Marvelous, infinite, matchless grace, freely bestowed on all who believe. You who are longing to see his face, will you this moment his grace receive?"

Prayer of reflection: Thank you, Lord, for your marvelous mercy and grace revealed in Christ Jesus. Help me today to share with others today those great gifts you have provided through Him.

My Prayer Journal

DAY 25

The Church of
The Holy Sepulcher

Theme: Hope
Read 1 Corinthians 15:12-28

IN HIS BOOK, *THE POWER TO CHANGE YOUR LIFE*, RICK WARREN tells about researchers at Cornell University who studied 25,000 prisoners from World War II. They concluded hope is the ingredient that enables a person to handle almost anything. No wonder Samuel Johnson wrote, "The natural flights of the human mind are not from pleasure to pleasure, but from hope to hope."

It was hopelessness that characterized the disciples of the Lord following the crucifixion. Yet because Jesus conquered life's greatest enemy on that first Easter, they were filled with hope.

A visit to the Church of the Holy Sepulcher depicts that hope. Pilgrims often stand in line for hours to get a glimpse of Calvary or the tomb which may have contained the body of the Risen Lord. Those locations are separated by only a few paces, but they reveal the gulf between hopelessness and hope.

I've often seen visitors lying on the ground weeping in those rooms. At first, that seemed like an odd reaction. Then I realized those

are not tears of sorrow. They are tears of joy and gratitude for all that Jesus has accomplished for us.

At the southern tip of Africa, there is a cape. When it was first discovered, it was called the Cape of Storms. Sailors feared to cross it because of the severity of the storms.

Vasco de Gama eventually ventured across those waters. For a few knots, he encountered turbulent storms, but not for long. Beyond the storms was a great calm. From then on, the area became known as the Cape of Good Hope.

That is what Jesus did to the grave. In fact, Paul argues that, if Christ is not alive, we have no hope. "And if Christ has not been raised, then your faith is useless and you are still guilty of your sins. But in fact, Christ has been raised from the dead. He is the first of a great harvest of all who have died" (1 Corinthians 15:17,20 NLT).

If Jesus is not alive, we have no hope for this world. The trajectory for this world continues down a steep decline without any hope for the future. But Jesus is alive! And "Because he lives, we can face tomorrow." We can overcome heartache, difficulties, adversity, and even death because the living Christ provides confidence that the grave is not final. He has conquered life's greatest enemy. There is hope for this life and the life to come because Jesus lives!

Peter summarizes all this: "Praise be to the God and father of our Lord Jesus Christ! In his great mercy he has given us new birth into a living hope through the resurrection of Jesus Christ from the dead, and into an inheritance that can never perish spoil or fade – kept in heaven for you" (1 Peter 1:3-5 NIV).

Prayer of reflection: Thank you, Lord, that I can face whatever comes in this world because you have conquered Life's Greatest Enemy.

My Prayer Journal

_____

_____

_____

_____

_____

_____

_____

_____

_____

_____

_____

_____

_____

_____

_____

_____

_____

_____

_____

_____

_____

_____

_____

DAY 26

The Garden Tomb

Theme: The Resurrection of Christ
Read Matthew 28:1-10

A FAVORITE SPOT FOR MANY CHRISTIANS WHO VISIT THE Holy Land is the Garden Tomb. Dozens of groups enjoy Communion each day in this peaceful setting in the middle of the noisy streets of Jerusalem and next to a bus station.

This beautiful garden provides a wonderful reminder of the resurrection of our Lord. The location includes a very old tomb, even though it may not be the original tomb of Jesus.

In fact, there are many empty tombs around Jerusalem because grave robbers have stolen the contents of those tombs over the centuries. Therefore, the greatest argument for the resurrection of Jesus is not an empty tomb, because there are many in this vicinity. The greatest argument for the resurrection of Jesus is that a dead man came out of one of those tombs and *appeared to His followers* who had seen him die.

Those followers feared Jewish and Roman authorities who might accuse them of being insurrectionists. Nearly all the followers of Jesus deserted Him when He died. Thomas even said, "Unless I see the

nail marks in his hands and put my finger where the nails were, and put my hand into his side, I will not believe" (John 20:24 NIV).

It didn't take long for the Resurrected Christ to meet that challenge. "A week later his disciples were in the house again, and Thomas was with them. Though the doors were locked, Jesus came and stood among them and said, 'Peace be with you!' Then he said to Thomas, "Put your finger here; see my hands. Reach out your hand and put it into my side. Stop doubting and believe." Thomas said to him, "My Lord and my God!" (John 20:26-28 NIV).

It's almost as if Jesus said to Thomas, "OK, big guy, let me prove that I'm alive. Go ahead and touch my hands and my side."

But that wasn't the only appearance of the Lord following His resurrection. 1 Corinthians 15 summarizes those appearances: "For what I received I passed on to you as of first importance: that Christ died for our sins according to the Scriptures, that he was buried, that he was raised on the third day according to the Scriptures, and that he appeared to Cephas, and then to the Twelve. After that, he appeared to more than five hundred of the brothers and sisters at the same time, most of whom are still living, though some have fallen asleep. Then he appeared to James, then to all the apostles, and last of all he appeared to me also, as to one abnormally born" (1 Corinthians 15:3-8 NIV).

It's one thing to die as a martyr for something you believe to be true. It's an entirely different thing to die for a lie. Those whimpering cowards were transformed into bold proclaimers of the Gospel all because of one thing: They saw a dead man walking! They were accused of "turning the world upside down" with their message because they had seen their crucified Lord alive.

The late Chuck Colson often told about his role in the Watergate scandal of the Nixon administration. As the secrets of Watergate unraveled, the President's closest advisers tried to deceive the American public about the truth. Even though they were charged with protecting the most powerful man in the world, they couldn't endure "living a lie" – even for a few weeks.

If the disciples of Jesus had only devised a plan to deceive others about Christ's apparent resurrection, how long do you think their little scheme would have lasted? How could they have faced martyrdom unless they had been radically changed by the post-resurrection appearance of the Man they saw die? For 2,000 years, their transformed lives have stood as a powerful testimony for the greatest miracle the world has ever witnessed!

Prayer of reflection: Thank you, Lord Jesus, that you conquered death through your resurrection. Help me to live in light of the "power of your resurrection."

My Prayer Journal

DAY 27

Mount of Ascension

Theme: Anticipation
Read Acts 1:1-11

A WHILE AGO, I MET MY WIFE, ROXANNE, AT AN AIRPORT following almost a month of separate traveling. Between our family needs and ministry responsibilities, we were eager to see each other again.

I still remember what it felt like to stand at the airport waiting to see her. Each time passengers would step off the tram from the secure area of the terminal, I got out of my chair to see if she was in that group. I checked the face of every passenger, longing to see my sweetheart. Even though we were about to celebrate our 42nd wedding anniversary, I must have looked like a teenager waiting for his girlfriend as I jumped up-and-down whenever a new tram arrived.

That experience reminds me of what occurred on the Mount of Olives following the resurrection of the Lord 2000 years ago. Just before Jesus returned to heaven, He gave his followers these instructions: "But you will receive power when the Holy Spirit comes upon you. And you will be my witnesses, telling people about me everywhere—in Jerusalem, throughout Judea, in Samaria, and to the ends of the earth." (Acts 1:8 NLT).

The great historian, Dr. Luke, details for us what happened next: "After saying this, he was taken up into a cloud while they were watching, and they could no longer see him. As they strained to see him rising into heaven, two white-robed men suddenly stood among them. 'Men of Galilee,' they said, 'Why are you standing here staring into heaven? Jesus has been taken from you into heaven, but someday he will return from heaven in the same way you saw him go!' (Acts 1:9-11 NLT).

Talk about an exit strategy! The Bible emphasizes that we should eagerly anticipate the return of Christ for us as His Bride. I love these words: "But our citizenship is in heaven. And *we eagerly await a Savior from there*, the Lord Jesus Christ" (Philippians 3:20 NIV).

You don't have to jump out of your chair every few minutes to "eagerly await" the return of Christ. But God does call us to live expectantly in light of His soon return.

Prayer of reflection: Thank you, Jesus, that you will return for your Bride someday. Please help me to live in light of how that return could happen today.

My Prayer Journal

The Southern Steps

Theme: The Holy Spirit
Read Acts 2:1-41

I LOVE WALKING IN AUTHENTIC PLACES IN ISRAEL. SO MUCH of the history of the land lies hidden beneath church buildings and

shrines built through the ages. Therefore, it's refreshing to walk along the shore of the Sea of Galilee and imagine Jesus preparing breakfast for his disciples. It's fascinating to climb the slopes of the Herodian and look down toward the fields where angels appeared to shepherds on the night of Jesus' birth.

I have that same feeling when I visit the Southern Steps of the Temple Mount. Nobody has built a shrine or a church there. Repairs have

been made to some of the steps, but many stones remain undisturbed since Jesus walked, taught, and performed miracles there.

It's not difficult to imagine throngs of people ascending those steps each year at one of three major Jewish festivals to offer their animals in sacrifice. Thousands of people would flock to Jerusalem from all over the world to celebrate the work of God during Passover, Pentecost, and Tabernacles.

One year at Pentecost, the Spirit of God did something miraculous on those steps. The Book of Acts tells us the disciples had gathered a few hundred yards away in the Upper Room following the resurrection of Jesus to "wait for the gift" he promised. Suddenly, the Holy Spirit came on them, a sound like a violent wind came from heaven, and tongues of fire appeared to rest on each of them.

They made their way toward the Temple and were supernaturally empowered to preach in foreign languages they had not previously known. People who had come from all over the world to offer sacrifices at the Temple in Jerusalem heard the disciples "declaring the wonders of God" in their own languages (Acts 2:11 NIV).

Finally, Peter raised his voice above the clamoring throng and proclaimed the truth about Jesus. 3000 people became followers of Christ that day, and the Church was born! The Bible even says that "those who accepted his message were baptized..." (Acts 2:41a NIV).

But wait... where did they get all the water for baptism? Archaeological excavations near the Southern Steps have revealed mikvahs, or ritual baths, that were used to prepare the people as they brought their animals to the temple. Apparently, those same ritual baths were used for baptizing new converts to Jesus Christ on the Day of Pentecost.

And here is better news... The same Spirit of God who empowered believers in those early days of the Church is available to you and me. Today, the Holy Spirit baptizes us into the body of Christ (1 Corinthians 12:13), seals us forever with the guarantee of our redemption (Ephesians 1:13–14) and convicts us of sin (John 16:8).

DAY 29

Old Jaffa

Theme: Evangelism
Read Acts 10:9-35

NO QUESTION ABOUT IT… THE PORT OF OLD JAFFA (BIBLICAL "Joppa") is a gorgeous place today. It's beautifully lit at night and picturesque in the daytime. I'm not sure it felt that way, however, to a couple of well-known biblical characters. In Joppa, both Jonah and Peter received a commission from God to proclaim His mercy and grace to hated heathens. Neither was crazy about the idea.

Jonah was supposed to preach repentance to the people of Nineveh, located northeast of Joppa, but in an act of defiance, he sailed northwest toward Tarshish

– the opposite direction. Eventually the rebel prophet was thrown overboard by his shipmates, started to drown and got a quick lesson in the digestive processes of some great fish. It's almost as if the fish thought, "I can't stomach this." All this convinced Jonah that maybe going to Nineveh wasn't such a bad idea after all.

Peter was also a devout Jew who believed that Gentiles were "unclean" and should be avoided at all cost. But God sent a vision of clean and unclean animals to him (Acts 10) to demonstrate that all men can be recipients of His love. Peter obediently headed to the house of Cornelius at Caesarea, where the Roman centurion was converted.

Both men learned that God is "no respecter of persons." The Gospel has the power to transform the life of anyone – regardless of racial, ethnic, religious, or moral background. The job of every believer is to evangelize. That doesn't mean we hit people over the head with the Bible. It simply means to share the Good News of God's love with those who are far from Him.

God has left us on this earth for that reason! Just as the "Son of Man came to seek and save those who are lost" (Luke 19:10), every child of God has a similar mission in this world. In fact, it's a rescue mission – much like a lifeguard rescues those who are drowning. Jesus said we are to "Go into all the world and preach the gospel to every creature" (Mark 16:15 NIV).

That means our primary concern in life should be the eternal destiny of those who are far from God. Our occupations are not the restriction. Our financial status is not the restriction. Our health is not even the restriction. The only restriction is whether we choose to accept that responsibility. To live on mission means we use every available resource to share the Good News of God's love with those who are perishing.

Prayer of reflection: Heavenly Father, people all around me today are headed to eternity apart from you. Help me to capture each encounter with the passion of a lifeguard who rescues a drowning person.

My Prayer Journal

DAY 30

The Mediterranean Sea

Theme: Risk & Reward
Read 2 Corinthians 11:21-30

THERE IS SOMETHING MESMERIZING ABOUT GENTLE WAVES that lap upon the sands of a beautiful beach. That constant repetition is almost hypnotic. It can easily lull you to sleep.

As I write these words I'm looking out a hotel room window in Tel Aviv at the beautiful blue waters of the Mediterranean. It's just gorgeous. Who doesn't prefer the repetitive calm of gentle waves to the back-breaking turbulence of storms on the water?

Just a few miles up the coast, the Apostle Paul sailed from the port of Caesarea for two of his missionary

journeys. But he didn't always enjoy the calm waters desired by most tourists to this area. Storms on the Mediterranean can pack a serious blow!

Paul reminds us of the adventures he encountered: "Three times I was beaten with rods. Once I was stoned. Three times I was shipwrecked. Once I spent a whole night and a day adrift at sea. I have traveled on many long journeys. I have faced danger from rivers and from robbers. I have faced danger from my own people, the Jews, as well as from the Gentiles. I have faced danger in the cities, in the deserts, and on the seas. And I have faced danger from men who claim to be believers but are not (2 Corinthians 11:25-26 – NLT).

Why? Why would Paul endure all of that? Was it just the adventure? No!

The risk was worth the reward! He writes to Timothy: "I have fought the good fight, I have finished the race, and I have remained faithful. And now the prize awaits me—the crown of righteousness, which the Lord, the righteous Judge, will give me on the day of his return. And the prize is not just for me but for all who eagerly look forward to his appearing" (2 Timothy 4:7-8 – NLT).

It's the same for you and me. Whatever we endure in this life for the cause of Christ will be worth it. He has a reward waiting for us that far outweighs any benefit in this life. "It will be worth it all, when we see Jesus! Life's trials will seem so small, when we see Christ. Once glimpse of His dear face, all sorrow will erase. So bravely run the race, till we see Christ."

Prayer of reflection: Today I ask you, Lord, for the grace to endure whatever hardships and difficulties I encounter knowing that someday I will be with you.

My Prayer Journal